A Primer of Beijing Opera

By Dr. Liang Yan

Foreign Languages Press

About the Author

Liang,Yan, associate professor of the Academy of Chinese Traditional Opera, received her Bachelor's degree in Chinese literature from Beijing Normal University in 1987, MA and Doctorate degrees from China's Academy of Arts in 1993, 1996. She is presently deputy Dean of Theatric Literature Department of ACTO and a tutor for MA candidates.

About the English Translator

RB Baron, of Albion,California, USA, received her Bachelor's degree in Modern Chinese History from the University of California--Santa Cruz in 1991.She has been dividing her time between China and the United States since 1991, and has translated a wide range of Chinese literary and scientific materials into English.

About the Photographer

Yu, Genquan, member of Chinese Association of Photographers, and of Chinese Association of Dancers, is a state-level senior photographer and presently works as the Director of the Center for Education & Technology at the PLA's Academy of Arts.

CONTENTS

Introduction

Shu Fang Zhai Imperial Theater in the Forbidden City, used exclusively for performances for the Emperor and the royal family during the Qing Dynasty.

When you open this book your first question may well be, "What exactly is Beijing opera?" Actually, the English term "Beijing opera" is somewhat misleading, in that it may cause Western readers to equate this unique Chinese dramatic art form with Western opera. A similar misunderstanding arises when Chinese acrobatics is referred to as "Chinese circus," equating it with Western circuses. Actually, the so-called "Chinese circus," with no animal acts, high wires, or trapeze work, is much more limited than Western circuses, which include all of these as well as acrobatics.Conversely, Beijing opera, which includes dance, dialogue, and martial arts, as well as music, is much more comprehensive than Western opera, which relies on singing as its primary means of expression. Beijing opera also transcends dance theater, in which gesture and movement provide the vehicle by which a story is told. And it surpasses traditional theater, which employs spoken dialogue to portray its characters and propel plot development. Beijing opera is a unique type of dramatic narrative, that weaves together music, movement, and dialogue to unfold beautiful and moving stories drawn from Chinese history, biography,

Introduction

13 most eminent Beijing Opera artists of the Qing Dynasty(1616 —1911 AD).

folk legend, literature. Its performers must be not only outstanding singers and actors, but also skilled in dance, acrobatics, and martial arts.

For thousands of years, Chinese society has been profoundly influenced by the thinking of the renowned Chinese philosopher Confucius (551-479 BC). The impact of Confucian ideology is apparent in China's politics, law, history, religion, philosophy, and social phenomenon. The extensive Beijing opera canon also clearly reflects the Confucian concern with ethics and morality. "Good and evil will receive their just rewards" is a common Chinese saying, and this outlook is fundamental to Beijing opera. There is no pure tragedy or comedy in Beijing opera. Rather, these two aspects of life are seen as inseparable, with the struggle between good and evil serving as the vehicle which carries each story to its morally unequivocal conclusion.

Beijing opera's appeal lies not only in the richness of its performances, but also in the diversity of its productions. Writers, composers, directors, and actors are all constantly changing. Although the basic stories remains the same, each production is unique in scenario, structure, vocal expression, and acting style. The twenty-six stories introduced in this book have been selected from the two hundred most frequently performed Beijing operas. They are divided into seven categories: stories of moral instruction, tales of loyalty and duty, historical pieces, stories of palace intrigue, legal cases, love stories, and legends about immortals. We hope that reading them will give you insight into both the lives and culture of the Chinese people. ∎

Types of Different Face-paint (Facial Make-up)

I Stories of Moral Instruction

The General and Prime Minister Reconcile Their Differences

> Origin:
> *Western Han Dynasty (206 BC - 25AD) historical compilation,*
> ***The Historical Records***
> Time:
> *Warring States Period (475-221 BC)*
> Place:
> *The State of Qin (present day Shaanxi Province)*
> *The State of Zhao (present day Hebei Province)*
> Main characters:
> *Lian Po (General of the State of Zhao)*
> *Lin Xiangru (Prime Minister of the State of Zhao)*

This story is set during China's Warring States Period (475-221 BC), a time when seven states are pitting their military might in a protracted contest for political hegemony. Of these states, Qin is the strongest, while Zhao is relatively small and weak. The King of the State of Qin learns that the State of Zhao possesses a priceless piece of jade known as the "He Family Tablet," and becomes determined to acquire it. He sends a messenger to Zhao, saying that he is willing to offer fifteen of his cities in exchange for this treasure. The King of Zhao, well aware of the King of Qin's reputation for craftiness, fears that he will renege on the bargain once the tablet is in his possession. He dispatches Lin Xiangru, a counselor of humble background, to take the treasure to Qin and uphold the dignity of Zhao.

The King of Qin is ecstatic when he lays eyes on the snow-white, glittering jade tablet. He clasps it possessively to his breast, but refuses to broach the subject of the fifteen cities he has promised in exchange. Lin Xiangru manages to retrieve the treasure from the King's

*Veteran general Lian Po, from **The General and Prime Minister Reconcile Their Differences.** Initially suspicious and narrow-minded, this painted face character rectifies his attitude when he realizes his mistake.*

grasp by pointing out a pretended flaw in the jade. Once he has the tablet in his hands, he sternly proclaims that the King of Qin's word is meaningless, and that he, Lin Xiangru, will smash the treasure and defy the King, even if it means his own death. Unable to justify himself, the King has no choice but to allow Lin Xiangru to depart, and the "He Family Tablet" is returned to the State of Zhao intact and unharmed. (This is the story behind the old Chinese saying "The tablet returns unharmed to Zhao"—to return something of value to its owner undamaged.)

After Lin Xiangru's return, the King of Zhao appoints him Prime Minister in recognition of his talents. General Lian Po, an old veteran of long-standing experience, is very displeased to see this young upstart elevated to such high position. He repeatedly accosts the new Prime Minister in the streets, obstructing his passage and subjecting him to public insult. Each time, Lin Xiangru steps aside and declines to engage in dispute.

"Bearing thorns to seek punishment," a scene from **The General and Prime Minister Reconcile Their Differences.** *Prime Minister Lin Xiangru is on the right.*

Lian Po becomes increasingly self-satisfied and arrogant when he sees Lin Xiangru acting in what he considers to be a weak and spineless manner. After deep reflection, Lin Xiangru sends a friend with a message to Lian Po. He begs the General to put the larger picture above personal considerations. He reminds him that the State of Qin, a ravening wolf at their borders, is poised to attack, and dissension between General and Prime Minister will deeply imperil the national security of Zhao.

Moved by this rational appeal, Lian Po is deeply ashamed of his behavior, and falls into a pit of self-reproach. One day he appears at Lin Xiangru's door, naked from the waist up and bearing thorny branches on his back, begging to be punished. (This is the origin of the Chinese saying "Bearing thorns to seek punishment"—to offer a humble apology.) Lin Xiangru embraces the old general, tears running down his face, and emotionally thanks him for his sincerity. Equally moved, Lian Po vows that from this moment on, General and Prime Minister will support each other to the death in the defense of their country, the State of Zhao. ■

Clear Wind Pavilion

Origin:

Ming Dynasty (1368-1644 AD) novel, **Clear Wind Pavilion**

Time:

Tang Dynasty (618-907 AD)

Place:

Southern China

Main characters:

Zhang Yuanxiu and his wife (poor city dwellers)

Zhang Jibao (their adopted son)

Zhang Yuanxiu and his wife, an old couple in their sixties, are returning home after enjoying the lanterns on Lantern Festival Eve. Suddenly they notice a wooden box on the street, the wailing of an infant emanating from within. The old man opens the box. Inside is a plump baby boy, shivering violently in the cold of the winter night. Taking the baby in her arms, the old woman discovers that he is wrapped in a piece of bloodstained white cloth. On the cloth is a message from the baby's mother, written in her own blood. The mother's name is Zhou Guiying, the concubine of a scholar named Xue Rong. She has just given birth to this son. Xue Rong is away taking the Imperial exams, and his primary wife, who never accepted Zhou Guiying, has accused the child of being a bastard. The wife has demanded that Zhou Guiying strangle the baby, her own flesh and blood. Afraid for her child's life, Zhou Guiying has no choice but to leave him on the street, in the hopes that some compassionate stranger will take him in. The kind-hearted old couple carefully fold away the message, and take the child home to raise, giving him the name Zhang Jibao.

Thirteen years later, Zhang Jibao has grown into a handsome young man. The old couple

*Zhang Yuanxiu and his wife prepare to greet their foster son, official Zhang Jibao, in **Clear Wind Pavilion.***

love him dearly, and work tirelessly plaiting straw shoes and making tofu, to earn money to allow him to study. One day, Zhang Jibao's birth mother arrives at their door, imploring them to give her back her son. She tells them that her husband has been granted an official post, and she wants to give her child a better life. The two old people think long and hard. Finally, in the interests of Zhang Jibao's future, they agree to let him go with his birth mother to the capital. Watching their beloved foster son depart is like a knife in their hearts. Soon they both fall ill with grief, and their lives become desolate and lonely.

Several years later the Zhangs, now in their eighties, learn that Zhang Jibao has achieved the exalted rank of Top Scholar. They set off for Clear Wind Pavilion, where he is resting on the way to his new post. Leaning on each other for support, the travel-stained and weary old couple finally arrives before their foster son,resplendent in his scarlet official's robes. They can't believe it when coldly he instructs his servants to throw these old beggars two hundred coppers, and remove them from his sight. The two old people gaze at this ungrateful wretch of a son, speechless and trembling with grief and anger. They pick up the two strings of coppers and fling them at him with all their might. Weeping, they cast themselves to their deaths at the foot of Clear Wind Pavilion's stone steps.

Shortly after, Zhang Jibao is struck dead by lightening while on the road to his new post.■

Water Spilled Before a Horse

Origin:

> *Ming Dynasty (1368-1644 AD) novel,* ***Lanke Mountain***

Time:

> *Western Han Dynasty (206 BC-25AD)*

Place:

> *Zhejiang Province*

Main characters:

> *Zhu Maichen (an impoverished scholar)*
> *Cui (his wife)*

On the slopes of emerald green Lanke Mountain lives a scholar named Zhu Maichen and his wife, surnamed Cui. Zhu Maichen is an honest and tolerant person, thoroughly devoted to his studies. Unfortunately, despite repeated efforts, he has been able to gain no preferment through the Imperial exams. Coming from an impoverished family, he has no choice but to make his living by cutting firewood on Lanke Mountain.

Cui has shared her husband's poor and simple life for many years. Gradually she becomes more and more dissatisfied, and her disposition worsens until she can't stand the sight of her impoverished, bookworm husband. Unable to counter her bitter, sarcastic complaints, Zhu Maichen silently bears his wife's discontent.

One freezing winter day, Cui nags Zhu Maichen to go up the mountain to cut more firewood, even though the air is thick with flying snow. His belly grumbling with hunger, he sets out, hoping that if he works harder and brings home more rice, maybe his wife will be happy. Little does he know that Cui has already sought out a matchmaker who has found her a new

husband, the well-to-do Carpenter Zhang. When Zhu Maichen returns home, Cui presents him with a divorce agreement, demanding that he sign. Grief-stricken, Zhu Maichen implores his wife to be patient just a little longer, ensuring her that their life will improve when he passes the Imperial exams and is granted a post. But Cui coldly tells him that even if he became a high official, she would rather beg in the streets than ask for his help. Zhu Maichen realizes that their years of marital affection mean nothing to her, and finally has no choice but to sign the papers.

*Zhu Maichen and his wife, surnamed Cui, in **Water Spilled Before a Horse.***

Not long after, Zhu Maichen is successful in the highest Imperial examination, and is appointed garrison commander. Cui is distraught when she hears the news—how can her common carpenter ever compare to a garrison commander, whose wife enjoys both high status and great wealth? She resolves to return to Zhu Maichen, and discard her current husband. Barefoot, with unbrushed hair and dirty face, Cui throws herself before Zhu Maichen and begs him to take her back. Zhu Maichen regards her from atop his tall, gallant steed. After brief consideration, he instructs his servant to spill a pan of water onto the dirt before his horse. He then tells Cui that if she can put the water back in the pan, he will agree to take her back. (This is the origin of the Chinese saying "Spilled water cannot be gathered up again.") Realizing that she has burned her bridges irreparably, Cui is so deeply shamed and disturbed that she goes mad.■

The Brocade Pouch

Origin:
> *Folk story*

Time:
> *Ancient time*

Place:
> *Shandong Province*

Main characters:
> *Xue Xiangling (daughter of a wealthy family)*
> *Zhao (daughter of a poor family)*

Xue Xiangling lives with her wealthy family in the city of Dengzhou, in today's Shandong Province. Intelligent and beautiful, she is her parents' only daughter. She's been spoiled since the day she was born, and has grown up willful and self-indulgent. It is the eighteenth day of the sixth lunar month, a day traditionally considered to be auspicious, and the day chosen by Xue Xiangling's parents and the matchmaker for her wedding. As Xue Xiangling prepares to leave for her new married life, her mother gives her a brocade pouch full of jewels and ornaments. The pouch is embroidered with a mythical creature thought to protect children and childbirth, and Xue Xiangling's mother tells her that she hopes she will soon have a child. Xue Xiangling bids her mother farewell and seats herself in the magnificent flower-bedecked bridal sedan chair, and surrounded by family and retainers, sets off for her new home.

Along the way, Xue Xiangling's party is overtaken by a sudden downpour, and takes shelter from the rain in the Spring and Autumn Pavilion by the side of the road. Before long, they are joined in the pavilion by another bridal party, also caught out in the rain. This bridal

*Virtuous woman character Xue Xiangling, the daughter of a wealthy family, sits in her bridal sedan chair in **The Brocade Pouch**.*

sedan is old and dilapidated, and the clothes of the attendants are little more than rags. The bride, surnamed Zhao, is also from Dengzhou. Her family is so poor that she has no servant to accompany her to her new home, and she fears that she will be mocked and abused by her new husband's family. When Zhao sees Xue Xiangling, with all her wealth and privilege, the comparison is too much for her to bear, and she bursts into bitter tears. Xue Xiangling hears the sobbing and peeks out through the curtains of her sedan chair. Seeing the scene before her, she is overcome with sympathy. She takes the brocade pouch and instructs her servant to give it to Zhao, but not to reveal her name.

Shortly the rain passes, and Xue Xiangling and her party continue along their way. Zhao watches them go, the jewel-filled pouch in her hands, filled with gratitude and wonder at the existence of someone of such wealth and generosity of spirit. How will she ever be able to repay this person, when she would not even leave her name?

Six years rush by, and a terrible flood destroys Xue Xiangling's husband's property. Destitute, Xue Xiangling makes her way to the city of Laizhou, where she finds work as a servant with a prosperous family named Lu. One day, she happens to see her old brocade pouch, enshrined in a secret room by Madame Lu! Through their subsequent conversation, Xue Xiangling learns that Madame Lu is none other than Zhao, the impoverished bride of so long ago, and Madame Lu recognizes her benefactress from the Spring and Autumn Pavilion. Faced with such vagaries of fate, the two young women are filled with deep emotion. Madame Lu repays her debt by bringing Xue Xiangling's entire household of more than twenty people to live in her home under her protection. ∎

II Tales of Loyalty and Duty

The Zhao Family Orphan

Origin:

Western Han Dynasty (206 BC-25 AD) historical   compilation,
The Historical Records

Time:

Spring and Autumn Period (770-476 BC)

Place:

The State of Jin (Present day Shanxi Province)

Main characters:

Cheng Ying (a village physician)

Zhao Wu (the Zhao family orphan)

Tu Anjia (general of the State of Jin)

General Tu Anjia of the State of Jin is cruel and merciless, bringing great harm to his country. He persecutes and falsely accuses the loyal and virtuous official Zhao Dun, and convinces the King of Jin to order the elimination of the entire Zhao family. In the course of one night, Zhao Dun and over three hundred members of his household, including his son Zhao Shuo, his relatives, and serving maids, are all murdered, their spirits rising from a sea of blood to wander the Earth as wronged and vengeful ghosts. Only Zhao Shuo's wife, Princess Zhuang Ji, the younger sister of the King of Jin, escapes with her life. Pregnant with Zhao Shuo's child, she is sent to live in seclusion in the King's inner palace.

Several months later, Princess Zhuang Ji gives birth to a son, whom she names Zhao Wu. This does not escape Tu Anjia's notice, and he orders that she and the baby be locked inside the inner palace. Princess Zhuang Ji is able to bring village physician Cheng Ying, an old friend of the Zhao family, into the palace on the pretext of illness, and tearfully begs him to save her son. Cheng Ying hides Zhao Wu in his medicine chest, and prepares to smuggle him out. Watch commander Han Jue, in deep admiration of Cheng Ying's righteousness, allows him to leave the palace with Zhao Wu, then killing himself with his own sword. Tu Anjia learns of the escape, but all his attempts to find the Zhao family orphan are unsuccessful. Furious, he orders the execution of all infants below the age of six months.

In order to protect the Zhao family orphan, and the lives of all the infants of the State of Jin, physician Cheng Ying and retired official Gongsun Chujiu devise a plan to deceive Tu Anjia. Cheng Ying replaces the Zhao family orphan with his own son and leaves him with Gongsun

Village physician Cheng Ying and Princess Zhuang Ji, in **The Zhao Family Orphan.**

Chujia, who will take the blame for rescuing and hiding the child. Cheng Ying personally goes to Tu Anjia, and denounces Gongsun as the culprit who is sheltering Zhao Wu. Convinced of the truth of Cheng Ying's charges, Tu Anjia viciously kills both the aged Gongsun and the false "Zhao family orphan." Commoners and officials alike are outraged at this cruel slaughter, but dare not voice their objections. Cheng Ying is cursed behind closed doors the length and breadth of the country, for betraying his friend in the pursuit of preferment. Cheng Ying stoically bears his grief and anger in the face of this vilification.

More than a decade goes by. Cheng Ying has spared no pains in raising Zhao Wu, who has grown into fine young man thoroughly versed in both the literary and martial arts. Cheng Ying arranges for Zhao Wu to be adopted by Tu Anjia, in order to position him to avenge his family. With the assistance of Wei Jiang, a commander just returned from the border, Zhao Wu finally confronts Tu Anjia. As he stabs his enemy, he reveals that he is none other than the heir that the General's merciless slaughter failed to eliminate—the Zhao family orphan.

In 1775, French author Voltaire published his translation of the Yuan Dynasty (1206-1368 AD) opera *The Revenge of the Zhao Family Orphan.* His work, entitled *The Chinese Orphan,* gained substantial recognition throughout Europe. ∎

The False Head and the Death of Tang

Origin:

Ming Dynasty (1368-1644 AD) story, **The Handful of Snow**

Time:

Ming Dynasty during the reign of Emperor Jiajing (1522-1566 AD)

Place:

Jiangsu Province

Main characters:

Mo Cheng (Mo Huaigu's vassal)

Xueyan (Mo Huaigu's concubine)

Tang Qin (Mo Huaigu's friend)

Treacherous official Yan Shifan learns that the wealthy Mo Huaigu possesses a rare and valuable treasure, a flawless white jade goblet known as "The Handful of Snow." Wanting it for himself, Yan Shifan submits a memorial to the Emperor falsely accusing Mo Huaigu of inciting rebellion. The Emperor, who is rather dense and easily led, issues an order that Mo Huaigu be executed on the spot, and his head brought to him in the capital.

News of the order reaches Mo Huaigu's home, and he flees by night. Vassal Mo Cheng is intensely loyal to his master Mo Huaigu, who once saved his life. Worried that Mo Huaigu will be captured and killed, Mo Cheng impersonates him and turns himself in to the local officials. Mo Cheng's head is accordingly cut off and sent to the capital. When Yan Shifan sees the head, he believes that Mo Huaigu is really dead, and calls off the pursuit.

Mo Huaigu's former friend Tang Qin, hoping for preferment, betrays the secret of the head to Yan Shifan. Yan Shifan immediately seizes Mo Huaigu's concubine, Xueyan, and subjects her to the third degree. In order to protect her husband's life, Xueyan resolutely maintains that the head really does belong to Mo Huaigu. Tang Qin, who has lusted after Xueyan for many years, secretly goes to her and says that if she agrees to marry him, he will convince Yan Shifan that the head is authentic. Xueyan is filled with loathing for this inhuman beast with the face of a man. But willing to die to protect her husband, she hides her revulsion and fury and pretends to agree to his demands.

Shi Qian, a Robin Hood-type Hero, is made a fighting clown character in Beijing Opera.

Tang Qin convinces Yan Shifan that Mo Huaigu actually is dead, and Xueyan is released. After their wedding ceremony, Tang Qin smugly carries Xueyan into the bridal chamber, where she plies him with wine until he is thoroughly befuddled. Then pulling out the dagger she has hidden in her robes, fiercely she stabs him again and again. Finally assured that her enemy is dead, she stabs herself and ends her own life.

Many years later, Yan Shifan falls from power, and Mo Huaigu finally returns from exile to his home.■

Su Wu Sent to Herd Sheep

> **Origin:**
> *Eastern Han Dynasty (25-220 AD) historical compilation,*
> ***The Book of the Han***
>
> **Time:**
> *Western Han Dynasty (206 BC-25 AD) during
> the reign of Emperor Han Wudi (140 - 87 BC)*
>
> **Place:**
> *China's northern frontier*
>
> **Main characters:**
> *Su Wu (envoy of the Western Han court)
> Hu A'yun (Su Wu's wife)*

During the time of the Western Han Dynasty (206 BC-25 AD), the Huns, a tribe of horse-riding nomads, regularly invade and plunder China's northern borderlands. When they threaten the safety of the capital, Chang'an, Emperor Han Wudi mounts a major expedition against them. After many years of bitter struggle, the human and material resources of the Western Han government are severely depleted, and the Emperor decides to attempt a diplomatic solution to the border problem. He dispatches young and promising mid-level official Su Wu as envoy to the Huns.

Su Wu bids farewell to his wife and mother, and holding the Han staff of office, departs with his retinue of over thirty people. After a trip of more than two months, they finally arrive at the capital of the Huns. Su Wu is granted an audience with the King of the Huns, Chan Yu. He tells Chan Yu that Emperor Han Wudi would like to foster cordial relations between their two countries, and hopes to reach an agreement to mutually lay down their arms. Chan Yu is very impressed by Su Wu's distinguished appearance and exceptional talents, and offers him high office and great wealth if he will defect to the Huns. Su Wu refuses in uncompromising terms. Chan Yu then sends two officials of the Western Han court who have already gone over to the Huns, Wei Lu and Li Ling, to Su Wu to try to persuade him. Su Wu curses both of them for betraying their monarch and their home. Stung by Su Wu's refusal, Chan Yu punishes him by sending him to Beihai to herd sheep.

Beihai is a vast and limitless field of dazzling ice, without a soul in sight. Su Wu subsists entirely on snow and coarse herbs, and stoically bears unimaginable loneliness. The Han staff of office in hand, he passes every day with only sheep for companions. Nineteen springs and autumns pass. Hu A'yun, daughter of the Hun commander in chief, is strongly attracted by the conduct and character of this man of the Han, and asks him to marry her. Su Wu, alone in a strange land, falls in love in his turn with this beautiful, passionate woman, who offers him such deep and intimate understanding. A year after their marriage, they give birth to a beautiful baby boy.

The Han government learns of Su Wu's detention, and his steadfast loyalty over the years. A great offensive is mounted against the Huns to rescue Su Wu and return him to court. Overmatched, the Huns agree to release Su Wu, but refuse to allow Hu A'yun or their child to accompany him back to the Han court. When the couple learns of this order, they embrace and sob long and bitterly. In order to fulfill her husband's dream of returning to his home, Hu A'yun entrusts their child to someone else, and kills herself with her sword. Su Wu, his heart full of grief and the Han staff of office still firmly in hand, returns to his homeland. ■

*Elder male character Su Wu, the Han envoy, holds his staff of office in **Su Wu Sent to Herd Sheep**. On the left is Hu A'yun, daughter of the Hun commander in chief, who later marries Su Wu.*

Wild Boar Forest

Origin:

    Ming Dynasty (1368-1644 AD) novel, **Outlaws of the Marsh**

Time:

    Later years of the Northern Song Dynasty (960-1127 AD)

Place:

    Northern China

Main characters:

    Lin Chong (commander of the Imperial Guard of the Northern Song court)

    Lu Zhishen (a monk and good friend of Lin Chong)

    Gao Qiu (a high minister of the Northern Song court)

Treacherous minister Gao Qiu has gained extensive power in court, and does as he pleases with no restraints. Gao Qiu's son, Gao Yanei, has fixed a lustful eye on the wife of Imperial Guard commander Lin Chong. Lin Chong's wife is as beautiful as

Lin Chong, banished to the Cangzhou hay yards in **Wild Boar Forest.**

the full moon and graceful as a flower, and Gao Yanei harasses her constantly with his licentious attentions. Lin Chong is furious, but unable to risk angering his superior Gao Qiu, is unable to retaliate.

In an attempt to gain preferment from Gao Qiu and his son, Lin Chong's friend Lu Qian suggests a scheme to eliminate Lin Chong. Lin Chong is summoned by Gao Qiu to bring his sword to court for a test of skill. When he arrives, he is tricked into entering White Tiger Hall, where important military strategy is discussed and no weapons are allowed. Gao Qiu then falsely accuses Lin Chong of plotting assassination, and has him banished to Cangzhou.

Unwilling to bring trouble upon his wife, Lin Chong writes a statement dissolving their marriage before he leaves, and urges her to remarry. But tearfully she swears that a thousand hardships and ten thousand dangers will not stop her from waiting for her husband's return.

Acting on orders from Gao Qiu, two of Lin Chong's guards prepare to murder him as they enter Wild Boar Forest. But Lin Chong's good friend, monk Lu Zhishen, appears like an avenger from Heaven, brandishing his staff and knocking the two thugs to the ground where they grovel for mercy.

When Lin Chong arrives at the Cangzhou prison camp, he is assigned to guard the army's supply of hay. One night, when the north wind is howling and the snow is flying, he goes out to buy some wine. When he returns, he discovers the hay yard ablaze, the flames leaping high into the sky. He takes shelter in a ruined temple to save himself, and overhears Lu Qian and several others boisterously talking and laughing. Lin Chong learns that his wife has committed suicide rather than submit to Gao Yanei, and that he himself is now to be killed. Unable to control his fury, he leaps forth with his sword and hacks his enemies to death. With no other path open to him, Lin Chong flees to Liang Mountain to join the resistance to Gao Qiu's control of the court.■

III Historical Pieces

Xi Shi

Origin:

Western Han Dynasty (206 BC-25 AD) historical compilation,
The Historical Records

Time:

Spring and Autumn Period (770-476 BC)

Place:

The State of Wu (present day Jiangsu Province)
The State of Yue (present day Zhejiang Province)

Main characters:

Xi Shi (a beautiful woman of Yue)
Fan Li (a minister of Yue)
Gou Jian (King of Yue)
Fu Chai (King of Wu)

Following their country's victory, beautiful Xi Shi and Minister Fan Li of the State of Yue decline reward and set sail on an outbound ship, in **Xi Shi**.

The neighboring states of Wu and Yue are historical enemies, constantly at war with each other. The State of Wu is extremely powerful, with superior military forces that have crushed the State of Yue to the point of extinction. After discussing the situation with his minister Fan Li, King Gou Jian of Yue informs King Fu Chai of Wu that he will submit to his authority and become his willing slave, in order to save his country.

King Fu Chai, flushed with victory, is delighted at the King of Yue's capitulation, and issues orders to cease all punitive actions against Yue. Gou Jian and his wife arrive at the court of Wu. They express their submission by cutting grass and working in the stables, while secretly dispatching people to drill their armies and restore the power of Yue. The State of Yue sends beautiful Xi Shi as a gift to the lascivious Fu Chai. When Fu Chai sees this woman with the face of a goddess, he becomes infatuated to the exclusion of all else. Spending his days and nights immersed in a haze of pleasure, he loses all interest in affairs of state. Xi Shi, on her part, follows the orders of the King of Yue to captivate the King of Wu with her charm and beauty, even though she and her countryman, the brilliant Minister Fan Li, are in love and engaged to be married. Masking her inner unwillingness and disgust, Xi Shi willingly pays this price to save her home of Yue.

After three years, the King of Yue sees that the State of Wu has exhausted its resources. Taking advantageof the situation, he initiates a major offensive against Wu. With its defenses severely weakened, Wu is unable to resist the attack. Fu Chai realizes that his country's situation is hopeless due to his actions, and filled with regret, kills himself in his palace.

The State of Yue vanquishes the State of Wu. King Gou Jian prepares to heap rich reward upon Fan Li and Xi Shi, but the two slip away onto an outbound ship, and with nary a farewell are lost from sight in the scintillating light of a mountain-ringed lake. ■

Farewell My Concubine

Origin:
> *Western Han Dynasty (206 BC-25 AD) historical compilation,*
> ***The Historical Records***

Time:
> *The last years of the Qin Dynasty (221-206 BC)*

Place:
> *Northern China*

Main characters:
> *Xiang Yu (overlord of the State of Chu)*
> *Yu Ji (Xiang Yu's concubine)*

Xiang Yu, overlord of the State of Chu, and Liu Bang, the King of Han, are engaged in a contest for supreme power over China. Xiang Yu is young and full of energy, valorous and militant. He has come close to death many times, but has never been vanquished. Liu Bang is more calculating, both resourceful and clever, with excellent advisors and generals under his command. Implementing his advisors' suggestions for defeating the arrogant overlord of Chu, Liu Bang joins forces with a number of regional commanders and surrounds Xiang Yu's base. After burning the grain and fodder stores of the Chu army, Liu Bang sends his counselor Li Zuoche to pretend to defect to Xiang Yu. Li Zuoche's instructions are to gain the trust of Xiang Yu and entice him away from his base, leaving him open to attack by the 300,000 strong force which awaits in ambush. True to form, the foolhardy Xiang Yu ignores the warnings of his advisors, and is taken in by Li Zuoche's blandishments. Rashly he leads his troops out of the base, and suffers overwhelming casualties.

Utterly defeated, Xiang Yu returns to camp, ashen and silent. His concubine Yu Ji does her

Imperial concubine Yu Ji performs a sword dance for overlord Xiang Yu after he returns to camp in defeat, in **Farewell My Concubine**.

best to put on a good face, offering him wine and words of comfort. Xiang Yu gazes at his beloved warhorse and this beautiful woman, and realizing that their remaining time together is very short, he starts to sing a bleak and solemn dirge. Donning her most beautiful robes and ornaments and brandishing a sword, Yu Ji dances and sings for her lord in an attempt to divert him from his troubles.

Late that night, the Han army surrounds the Chu encampment, singing the folksongs of the State of Chu in order to destroy the morale of the soldiers. (This is the origin of the Chinese saying "Surrounded by the songs of Chu" —to be besieged on all sides.) Like a bird paralyzed with fear at the twang of a bowstring, the Chu army loses all heart to do battle. Yu Ji urges Xiang Yu to break out of the encirclement, and return home to regroup and plan a new campaign. She then draws her sword and cuts her throat, to relieve Xiang Yu of all responsibility for her safety.

After a night of bloody slaughter, Xiang Yu finally breaks out of Liu Bang's trap. Alone, he comes to the banks of the river. As he gazes out at the raging torrent, he is unable to face the thought of returning home to tell his family of his losses. Filled with unbearable regret, he pushes his beloved steed into the torrent, and cuts his own throat.■

Cao Cao Captured and Released

Origin:

    Ming Dynasty (1368-1644 AD) novel,

    Romance of the Three Kingdoms

Time:

    Last years of the Eastern Han Dynasty (25-220 AD)

Place:

    Northern China

Main characters:

    Cao Cao (a minister of the Eastern Han court)

    Chen Gong (a county official)

    Lu Boshe (a friend of Cao Cao's father)

High official Dong Zhuo has seized power at court, bringing great misfortune to the people and disaster to the country. He is passionately hated by commoners and officials alike, but his power is so great that no one dares to move against him. Ambitious minister Cao Cao unsuccessfully attempts to assassinate Dong Zhuo, and an order is put out for his arrest. He flees, but when he reaches the county seat he is captured by the local officials. County official Chen Gong interrogates Cao Cao, and is deeply impressed by his fearless attempt to rid the country of the evil sycophant Dong Zhuo. Under Cao Cao's urging, Chen Gong decides to renounce his official post and join him in roaming the country, attempting to improve the people's lot.

On their way out of the city, the two encounter Cao Cao's father's good friend Lu Boshe. The old gentleman is delighted to see them, and warmly welcomes them into his home. Wanting to give his guests nothing but the best, Lu Boshe instructs his servants to kill a pig and sheep, and personally goes out to buy some wine. While Cao Cao is waiting with Chen Gong for Lu Boshe to return, he suddenly hears the sound of knives being sharpened.

Mistrustfully thinking that the Lu family is plotting to murder him, Cao Cao sets about with his sword, indiscriminately cutting down everyone in the house. In moments, more than a dozen members of Lu Boshe's household lie dead on the ground. Chen Gong, deeply shaken by Cao Cao's actions, has no idea of how to react. He goes into the kitchen where he sees the bound pig and sheep. Realizing the knives were meant for them, he reviles Cao Cao for mistaking Lu Boshe's good intentions, and killing so many innocent people. Cao Cao hurriedly pulls Chen Gong out the door, and they jump on their horses and flee.

Cao Cao and Chen Gong haven't gone far when they meet Lu Boshe on his way home with the wine. The old man tries to convince them to stay, but Cao Cao is adamant that he must depart. Chen Gong, afraid that Cao Cao will explode into violence once more, hastily urges Lu Boshe to return home. But before the old man gets very far, Cao Cao reconsiders, and turning his horse, goes galloping back and stabs his father's good friend to death. Chen Gong looks at the old man lying in a pool of blood, and demands of Cao Cao how he could be so cruel. Cao Cao bluntly replies that Lu Boshe might have sought revenge for his family, so it was best to eliminate him in order to avoid future trouble.

Late that night, Cao Cao's sleep is deep and untroubled, but Chen Gong cannot stop tossing and turning. He realizes that although Cao Cao may have a hero's determination, he is also excessively paranoid, crafty, and cruel. Determined to no longer associate with such a person, Chen Gong stealthily leaves Cao Cao's side.■

Treacherous official Cao Cao. His white face paint indicates his sly and deceitful nature.

Women Generals of the Yang Family

Origin:

> *Ming Dynasty (1368-1644 AD) novel,*
> ***Romance of the Yang Family Generals***

Time:

> *Northern Song Dynasty (960-1127 AD) during the reign*
> *of Emperor Song Renzong (1023-1063 AD)*

Place:

> *Northern China*

Main characters:

> *She Taijun (widow of a Song general)*
> *Mu Guiying (wife of She Taijun's grandson)*

The Western Xia regime (1038-1227 AD) has been making forays on China's northern borderlands for many years. Over the generations, more than a dozen generals and commanders of the Yang family have sacrificed themselves in defense of the lands of the Song Dynasty. She Taijun, the matriarch of the Yang family, is over one hundred years old, vigorous and highly skilled in the martial arts. Her husband and sons have all lost their lives in battle on the border. Every day she tirelessly leads her daughters, daughters-in-law, and great grandchildren in stringent military training.

One day, the Yang home is strung with festive lanterns and colored pennants. She Taijun is celebrating the fiftieth birthday of her beloved only grandson, Yang Zongbao. The feast is just getting underway, when border guard commanders Meng and Jiao come rushing in. Deeply distressed, they report that Yang Zongbao has fallen in battle. In the blink of an eye, cries of grief fill the air, and the banquet hall is transformed into a hall of mourning.

*Photograph of performance of **Women Generals of the Yang Family**.*

The ministers and officials of the Song court are not in agreement concerning the proper response to the incursions of the Western Xia. Minister Kou Zhun, representing the hawks, and Minister Wang Hui, representing the doves, argue heatedly in front of Emperor Song Renzong. The Emperor, weak and with no opinion of his own, appeals to numerous civil and military officials for advice on how to deal with this threat. But the entire court remains silent. When She Taijun hears about this, she appears in court leading twelve women generals, including her daughters, daughters-in-law, and granddaughter-in-law, and demands to be sent to the front. The Emperor is deeply impressed, and appoints She Taijun as supreme commander of the campaign against the Western Xia.

The Yang family women generals arrive at the border, and in their first engagement utterly rout the defending troops of the Western Xia. Even so, when the King of the Western Xia learns that his opponents are a group of women, he can't stop laughing. He concocts a scheme to lure She Taijun's forces into a mountain valley, and wipe them all out in one blow.

Yang Zongbao's widow, Mu Guiying, risks life and limb to scout the valley. Encountering

Courageous and militant woman general Mu Guiying, a martial woman character.

an old person gathering herbs, she learns the location of a concealed plank path suspended along the cliff. Late at night, like celestial soldiers and immortal generals, the women materialize at the rear of the Western Xia encampment. Catching the enemy unawares, they achieve an extraordinary victory. Raging fire consumes the enemy camp and illuminates the valley. The Yang family women generals exalt in their success, the triumph on their faces reflected in the leaping flames. ■

IV Stories of Palace Intrigue

Heaven's Blade

> Origin:
>> Western Han Dynasty (206 BC-25 AD) historical compilation,
>> **The Historical Records**
>
> Time:
>> Qin Dynasty (221-206 BC) during the reign of
>> Emperor Qin Ershi (209-207 BC)
>
> Place:
>> Xianyang (in present day Shaanxi Province)
>
> Main characters:
>> Zhao Yanrong (daughter of Qin minister Zhao Gao)
>> Zhao Gao (minister of the Qin court)

Incompetent Emperor Qin Ershi has placed treacherous minister Zhao Gao in a position of great authority, and the government is in chaos. One day, in order to flaunt his power to the assembled court officials, Zhao Gao brazenly mocks the Emperor by convincing him that a deer is really a horse. (This is the origin of the Chinese saying "Calling a deer a horse" — to deliberately misrepresent something.) Everybody is aware of Zhao Gao's malevolent trick, but can only watch in pained silence. But loyal and upright minister Kuang Hong cannot repress his indignation, and confronts Zhao Gao on the spot. Nursing his resentment, Zhao Gao seeks an opportunity to get revenge.

Kuang Hong has done battle for the Qin Dynasty the length and breadth of the land. To reward him for his meritorious service, the Emperor has personally given him a sword known as "Heaven's Blade." This is a great honor for Kuang Hong's family, and they consider the sword a family treasure to be handed down to future generations. Scheming to

*Zhao Yanrong, a virtuous woman character, feigns insanity in **Heaven's Blade**.*

frame Kuang Hong, Zhao Gao secretly has this sword stolen and placed in the Imperial palace. He then submits a memorial accusing Kuang Hong of plotting to kill the Emperor. Emperor Qin Ershi is furious, and orders the extermination of Kuang Hong's entire family.

Kuang Hong's son Kuang Fu flees to the border with the help of a servant. Kuang Fu's wife, Zhao Yanrong, is spared because she is Zhao Gao's beloved daughter, and is taken to live at her father's residence. Zhao Yanrong is deeply distressed by her father's actions, and passes her days in deep depression.

One evening, Emperor Qin Ershi makes an incognito visit to his minister's residence. When he sees Zhao Yanrong, with a figure like a willow and face like a peach, he is seized with urgent desire, and orders Zhao Gao to have her brought to his palace at once. Ignoring his daughter's vehement opposition, Zhao Gao informs her that she will be presented to the Emperor the following morning. Late that night, Zhao Yanrong's mute maid, communicating to her with gestures, helps her to tear her clothes, cast off her embroidered slippers, and tear loose her hair. Her face covered with bloodstains, Zhao Yanrong throws herself in front of her father, wildly cursing and reproaching Heaven and Earth. Zhao Gao is dismayed to see his daughter apparently insane, and has no choice but to inform the Emperor. Qin Ershi doesn't believe him, and insists on seeing for himself.

The next day, Zhao Yanrong is led by her maid into the Emperor's presence. Boldly she strides up the stairs of the Emperor's dais, where no one is allowed to set foot. Standing before the entire court, she curses as if she has taken leave of her senses, calling down imprecations on evil, immoral officials and bitterly rebuking Zhao Gao for his shameless, vicious actions. The lustful Emperor Qin Ershi is forced to feign disinterest in this crazy woman, and hastily ends the audience. Zhao Yanrong, fully prepared to die, descends from the dais, and lets out her breath in disgust.■

Beijing opera character General Gao Chong. His costume is a stylized version of the battle armor worn by generals in classical China.

The Drunken Beauty

Origin:
Ming Dynasty (1368-1644 AD) novel,
Wiping Clean the Mirror

Time:
Tang Dynasty (618-907 AD) during the reign of Emperor Tang Minghuang (712-756 AD)

Place:
Chang'an (in present day Shaanxi Province)

Main characters:
Yang Guifei (Imperial concubine of the Tang Emperor)
Gao Lishi (chamberlain of the Tang court)

Emperor Tang Minghuang, greatly enamored of wine, women, and song, dispatches his chamberlain, eunuch Gao Lishi, to conduct a search for the most beautiful women of the land. Gao Lishi tours the length and breadth of the country, and selects for the Emperor an exceptional beauty named Jiang Caiping. Not only is her face ethereal and her body like a swaying willow, but she is intelligent and creative as well, accomplished in both poetry and song. Tang Minghuang is well pleased when he sees her, and holds a lavish banquet to reward his officials. Because Jiang Caiping especially loves plum blossoms, the Emperor causes a plum orchard to be planted for her inside the rear palace walls, and gives her the name "Plum Concubine."

Before long, Tang Minghuang learns that his son Prince Shou has a concubine of even greater beauty, named Yang Yuhuan. He orders that she be sent to his palace to wait upon him. Prince Shou dares not disobey his father, and has no choice but to comply. Tang Minghuang receives Yang Yuhuan and inspects her closely, deciding that she is indeed the

*The Emperor's beloved concubine Yang Yuhuan, a virtuous woman character in **The Drunken Beauty**.*

most lovely woman under heaven. On the spot, he grants her the rank of "Guifei," or Imperial Concubine. From that moment on they are always together, soaking in hot springs, feasting and drinking on balmy spring nights, viewing flowers and listening to music, and singing and dancing.

One day, Tang Minghuang remembers the Plum Concubine, whom he has neglected for so long. He decides on the spot to go spend the night with her. Yang Yuhuan, unaware, sets out a feast of wine and delicacies in Hundred Flower Pavilion, and prepares to spend yet another night of pleasure with the Emperor. When the hours go by and the Emperor does not arrive, Yang Yuhuan realizes that there must be another woman in his heart. Assailed with a wave of bitter pain and resentment, she starts to drink alone, attempting to drown her sorrows while reflecting upon the transience of life and the unreliability of a man's heart. The more she drinks, the lower her spirits fall, until finally she is overcome by the wine and becomes totally inebriated. Gao Lishi, waiting by her side, attempts to console her, deeply sympathetic to this lonely, abandoned Imperial concubine. Yang Yuhuan waits until the moon sinks in the west and the stars fade, but the Emperor never comes. Finally she is supported home, drunk, staggering, and alone. ■

A Leopard Exchanged for a Prince

Origin:
> *Yuan Dynasty (1206-1368 AD) opera,* **The Makeup Box**

Time:
> *Northern Song Dynasty (960-1127 AD)*

Place:
> *Dongjing (in present day Henan Province)*

Main characters:
> *Concubine Liu (Northern Song Empress)*
>
> *Concubine Li (Imperial concubine of the Northern Song Emperor)*
>
> *Chen Lin (a palace eunuch)*
>
> *Kou Zhu (a palace maid)*
>
> *Zhao Heng (Northern Song Emperor)*
>
> *Zhao Zhen (Zhao Heng's son)*

Performance photograph from **A Leopard Exchanged for a Prince**.

Emperor Zhao Heng is over fifty years old. He has decided to designate his heir, but has not yet made his final choice. As it happens, Imperial concubine Li of the Eastern Palace and Imperial concubine Liu of the Western Palace become pregnant one after the other. Zhao Heng announces that whoever first presents him with a prince will be named Empress. Liu is distraught when she learns of this; she became pregnant well after Li, and her chances of giving birth first are almost nonexistent. Liu, however, is well versed in palace intrigue. She seeks out Chief Eunuch Guo Huai, and together they devise a scheme to prevent Li from becoming Empress.

The day comes that Li gives birth to a son. As the midwife is leaving the birthing chamber, she is stabbed to death and dragged away. A skinned leopard is substituted for the newborn infant, and presented to Emperor Zhao Heng. Liu tells the Emperor that Li has given birth to a monster, a very inauspicious omen for the palace. Zhao Heng, stupid and easily deceived, orders Li locked up in solitary confinement, and names Liu Empress.

Palace maid Kou Zhu is given a secret order to cast a sealed wooden makeup box into the river. But when she hears an infant's cries emanating from inside the box, she becomes suspicious and opens it. She discovers a boy baby inside, and not knowing what to do, goes to eunuch Chen Lin for help. Chen Lin, well aware of the struggle between the concubines of the Eastern and Western Palaces, realizes that this infant is none other than the prince to whom Li has just given birth. He manages to smuggle the baby out of the palace, and brings him to the palace of Emperor Zhao Heng's younger brother, Prince Baxian. The honest and upright Prince Baxian takes in the prince and raises him as his own, giving him the name Zhao Zhen.

When Liu's pregnancy is in its sixth month, the fetus dies in her womb. Zhao Heng has no choice but to choose his heir from among his relatives. Impressed by the stolid and heroic appearance of Prince Baxian's young son Zhao Zhen, he names him heir. When Liu notices Zhao Zhen's uncanny resemblance to Li, she becomes suspicious. She tortures serving maid Kou Zhu to extract a confession, but Kou Zhu remains silent to the death. Liu fears that Li, locked away in solitary confinement, will stage a comeback, and has her palace burned to the ground. Loyal and honest eunuch Chen Lin helps Li escape, and Liu has him beaten and tortured. Furious, Prince Baxian bursts into the palace and reveals to the Emperor the truth about Zhao Zhen. Zhao Heng is old and feeble, and the shock is too much for him. He dies on the spot, and Liu is once more in sole control of the court.

Several years later, Zhao Zhen ascends the throne. A blind old woman appears at court, claiming that she is the new Emperor's natural mother, and causing a great stir among officials and commoners alike. Respected judge Bao Gong investigates the case, realizing that it is very serious and the Empress may be involved. When Empress Liu learns that Bao Gong is seeking out all possible witnesses, she poisons loyal eunuch Chen Lin to prevent him from giving evidence. But Bao Gong uncovers the truth from his interrogation of Chief Eunuch Guo Huai and Prince Baxian's testimony concerning the prince's background. Liu, realizing that her evil deeds can no longer be concealed, hangs herself in her palace.

Bao Gong and Prince Baxian bring Zhao Zhen and Li together to meet. The Emperor prostrates himself before his mother, the true Empress Dowager, and mother and son fall into each other's arms weeping. ■

V Legal Cases

Snow in June

Origin:	
	Eastern Han Dynasty (25-220 AD) historical compilation, **The Book of the Han**
Time:	
	Ancient time
Place:	
	Northern China
Main characters:	
	Dou E (a young widow)
	Cai Po (Dou E's mother-in-law)
	Dou Tianzhang (Dou E's father)
	Zhang Lu'er (a local hoodlum)

In Shanyang County of the region of Chuzhou lives a scholar with a bellyful of learning named Dou Tianzhang. Unfortunately, his wife has died, leaving him and his young daughter Dou E with only each other to depend on. Widow Cai Po inherited her husband's estate when he died, and lives off the interest she makes from lending money. Dou Tianzhang once borrowed twenty taels of silver from her, and has never been able to repay the debt. The time comes when he must travel to the capital for the Imperial exams. Penniless and with no other options before him, he offers his daughter Dou E to Cai Po as a child bride for her son. Cai Po accepts, giving Dou Tianzhang back the receipt from his loan and several taels of silver for his expenses on the road.

Dou Tianzhang leaves Chuzhou, and no further word is heard from him. Springs come and autumns go, and summer's heat and winter's cold. Dou E grows into a young woman in Cai Po's home, and her marriage with Cai Po's son is celebrated. But after only three years, Dou E is widowed, leaving her and her mother-in-law to care for each other and together go through life. Local hoodlum and lay-about Zhang Lu'er wants to take Dou E as his wife, but

*Dou E is taken under guard to the execution grounds in **Snow in June**.*

is met with refusal. Believing that Cai Po is standing in the way of his marriage, he tries to poison her, but inadvertently kills his own mother instead. Zhang Lu'er threatens to charge Dou E with killing his mother unless she agrees to marry him. Dou E, naively placing her trust in the government, goes with Zhang Lu'er to the head of Shanyang County to clear her name. But without giving her a chance to defend herself, this corrupt official tortures her to force her to confess that she killed Zhang Lu'er's mother. In order to prevent her mother-in-law from also being tortured, Dou E confesses to the false charge, and is sentenced to death.

Brought to the execution grounds, Dou E wrathfully calls upon Heaven and Earth to bear witness to her innocence. As she is about to be beheaded, she swears three oaths to prove that she has been wronged. First, she vows that her hot and innocent blood will splash upon the white cloth hanging high above her. Second, a terrible blizzard will descend during the heat of June. And third, Shanyang County will suffer three years of drought. After Dou E's death, all three of her vows come to pass.

Dou E's father has long since passed the Imperial examinations and been granted a high government post. One day while he is reviewing court cases, he discovers the record of the false accusation against his daughter and her unjust execution. He reopens the case, and during the course of his inquiry discovers that the true criminal is Zhang Lu'er. Zhang Lu'er is beheaded, and the corrupt official whom he bribed is punished for his misuse of office and torture of the innocent.■

Four Top Scholars

Origin:
  Folk story
Time:
  Ming Dynasty (1368-1644 AD) during the reign of Emperor Jiajing (1522-1566 AD)
Place:
  Henan Province
Main characters:
  Song Shijie (a retired clerk)
  Yang Suzhen (a village woman)
  Mao Peng (a minister of the Ming Dynasty)

Tian Lun, Gu Du, Liu Ti, and Mao Peng are four top scholars who pass the highest level Imperial examination in the same year. Unhappy with corrupt government and officials who accept bribes and pervert the law, the four friends go together to a temple and swear an oath to uphold honest and righteous government, and never to give consideration to personal relationships.

Years later, Tian Lun's older sister poisons her husband's brother in an attempt to acquire his family's wealth. The murdered man's widow, Yang Suzhen, goes to court to bring charges, but Tian Lun's sister bribes the local official, her brother's old friend Liu Ti, and no one will pursue the case.

Tian Lun's sister fears that Yang Suzhen will refile her complaint, and sells her to a distant town. Yang Suzhen, friendless and alone, is exploited and maltreated until she is taken in by old retired clerk Song Shijie. Song Shijie, a kind and righteous man, adopts Yang Suzhen as his daughter, and brings charges on her behalf. County official Gu Du learns that Song Shijie is publicly agitating for Yang Suzhen. Knowing that this is not the first time the old man has intervened for others, Gu Du does everything he can to thwart him. But Song Shijie, thanks to his experience as a clerk in the Ministry of Punishments, is able to articulately press his case, and forces Gu Du to bring Tian Lun's sister in for questioning.

Tian Lun's sister arrives and gives Gu Du a letter from his old friend Tian Lun requesting special consideration, and three hundred taels of silver. Gu Du has Yang Suzhen tortured until she confesses to false charges. When Song Shijie exposes Gu Du's bribe taking and corrupt

Elder male character Song Shijie, in **Four Top Scholars**.

activities, Gu Du furiously orders that he receive forty heavy blows with the cudgel, a punishment he surely will not survive. Filled with righteous indignation, Song Shijie stops the sedan chair of touring minister Mao Peng, crying out that he has been wronged. When Mao Peng sees the local officials closing ranks to protect each other, and the suffering of the people that fills the land, he realizes that the oath the four friends took together has become no more than empty words. He determines to conduct a thorough legal investigation, and get to the bottom of this case.

In the end, Tian Lun's villainous sister is arrested and brought to justice. The three corrupt officials, Tian Lun, Liu Ti, and Gu Du, are removed from their posts and punished. And Song Shijie and Yang Suzhen are cleared of all charges and given their freedom. ■

Qin Xianglian

Origin:

> *Folk story*

Time:

> *Northern Song Dynasty (960-1127 AD)*

Place:

> *Dongjing (in present day Henan Province)*

Main characters:

> *Qin Xianglian (Chen Shimei's wife)*
> *Chen Shimei (a scholar of the Song Dynasty)*
> *Bao Gong (a judge of the Song Dynasty)*

Chen Shimei, a scholar from Jingzhou, travels to the capital for the Imperial examinations, leaving his aged parents and young son and daughter home in the care of his wife, Qin Xianglian. Three years pass with no word from Chen Shimei. Jingzhou is struck by a severe drought, the crops fail, and Chen Shimei's father and mother die of cold and hunger. After Qin Xianglian buries her parents-in-law, she takes her children and sets out to the capital in search of her husband.

Mother and children travel without stopping for many days, and finally, hungry and tired, arrive in the capital and stop at an inn. They learn from the innkeeper that after Chen Shimei passed the highest Imperial examination three years ago, he attracted the interest of the Empress Dowager, and is now married to the Princess. Qin Xianglian, furious at the news, bursts into Chen Shimei's palace and confronts him. Chen Shimei, unwilling to jeopardize his high position and great wealth, has Qin Xianglian and the two children thrown out the door.

Qin Xianglian sees Prime Minister Wang Yanling's sedan chair passing through the busy city streets, and jumps in front of it to halt its progress. She kneels down in front of the Prime Minister, and appeals for his help in bringing suit against Chen Shimei. Wang Yanling realizes that this is a matter of national importance, involving the royal family, and hopes to resolve it without a public court case. He has Qin Xianglian disguise herself as a musician, and attempt to appeal to Chen Shimei's conscience by singing a song about a similar family's suffering. But Chen Shimei's suspicions are aroused, and he recognizes Qin Xianglian. Believing that she has been sent to deliberately humiliate him, he kicks and beats her mercilessly, and has her forcibly evicted. When Wang Yanling sees Chen Shimei's unrelenting cruelty and heartlessness, he advises Qin Xianglian to appeal to the illustrious, influential Judge Bao Gong.

Late at night, Qin Xianglian and the two children are ambushed by a knife-wielding assassin, who has been employed by Chen Shimei to kill them. They beg for mercy, telling him that they are Chen Shimei's wife and children. The assassin realizes that Chen Shimei is a beast in human form, and cannot bring himself to kill these wronged and innocent people. Knowing that he will not be able to explain his failure to carry out his mission, the assassin ends his own life. Qin Xianglian, shaking with anger, seizes the bloody knife and goes to Judge Bao Gong to declare her grievance against Chen Shimei. Bao Gong determines that Chen Shimei has attempted to kill his own wife and children, and if not stopped will continue to persecute them until they are dead. He rules that he must be punished. Chen Shimei appeals to the Empress Dowager, and the Princess appears to plead on his behalf. But the uncompromisingly ethical Judge Bao Gong does not waver,even knowing that he risks dismissal or worse. Resolutely, he sentences Chen Shimei, who has abandoned all honor and decency, to be beheaded.■

Judge Bao Gong, also known as Bao Zheng, in **Qin Xianglian**. *His black face paint indicates his impartiality, incorruptibility, and integrity.*

VI Love Stories

Stories from a Girl's Room

Origin:

Tang Dynasty (618-907 AD) novel, **The Story of Yingying**

Time:

Tang Dynasty (618-907 AD)

Place:

Puzhou (in present day Shanxi Province)

Main characters:

Zhang Hong (an unemployed scholar)

Cui Yingying (daughter of the Prime Minister)

Hong Niang (a maid in the Cui household)

Zhang Hong is a gifted scholar, but not yet having found an outlet for his talents, he wanders wherever his fancy takes him. He arrives in the town of Puzhou, and takes shelter at Pujiu Temple. Cui Yingying and her mother are returning from their hometown, where they have just buried Yingying's father, the recently deceased Prime Minister. Passing through Puzhou, they decide to stay at Pujiu Temple for a time. One day, Yingying and her maid Hong Niang encounter Zhang Hong in the Hall of the Great Buddha, where he is engaged in conversation with the old chief monk who runs the temple. Yingying and Zhang Hong fall in love at first sight.

Zhang Hong's room is right next door to Cui Yingying's. He writes her poems under the moonlight, and serenades her with his lute in the garden full of flowers. Yingying is enraptured. Suddenly one day, bandit chief Sun Feihu lays siege to Pujiu Temple with a force of 3,000 mounted soldiers. He demands that the chief monk hand over Cui Yingying to be his wife in his mountain stronghold, or he will burn the temple to the ground. Panicked,

From right to left: Cui Yingying, her maid Hong Niang, and scholar Zhang Hong,
*in **Stories from a Girl's Room**.*

Yingying's mother Madame Cui announces that she will give Yingying in marriage to anyone who can repel the bandit forces. Hearing this, Zhang Hong leaps forward and asserts that he has a plan. He dashes off a letter to his friend, General Bai Ma, asking him to come with his troops to break the siege. Monk Huiming bravely volunteers to carry the message, and makes his way out through the encirclement. General Bai Ma arrives on schedule and utterly routs the bandits, and peace returns once more to Pujiu Temple.

Several days later, Zhang Hong is invited to a great banquet by the Cui family. But during the festivities, Madame Cui goes back on her word, telling Zhang Hong that he should seek a wife elsewhere. Zhang Hong, Cui Yingying, and Hong Niang are deeply upset at this turn of events. Zhang Hong falls ill and takes to his bed, and Yingying is bitterly resentful of her mother's ingratitude. Zhang Hong and Yingying are immersed in longing for each other. Hong Niang thinks it's all very unfair, and helps Zhang Hong by delivering his love letters to Yingying. But Yingying, afraid that Hong Niang might reveal their secret, acts alternately warm and cold, until Zhang Hong isn't sure what she really feels. One night, Yingying manages to secretly visit Zhang Hong, and the two passionately declare their love for each other.

Madame Cui eventually gets wind of the secret love affair, and demands an explanation from Hong Niang. Hong Niang, filled with righteous indignation, rebukes Madame Cui for breaking her promise and betraying people's trust, and urges her to let Yingying and Zhang Hong marry. Worried that her dishonorable conduct might become public, Madame Cui has no choice but to agree. But she requires that Zhang Hong first pass the Imperial exams in the capital and be granted a high government post.

Yingying goes to see Zhang Hong off at Ten Mile Pavilion. Heartbroken at being parted, she tearfully begs him to come back soon. Six months go by, and Zhang Hong returns with the news that he has failed the Imperial exams. Madame Cui rudely throws Zhang Hong out, and promises her nephew Zheng Heng that he may marry Yingying. Yingying is enraged at her mother's heartlessness. That night she and Hong Niang pack their bags and slip away from Pujiu Temple in pursuit of Zhang Hong. Zhang Hong has stopped for the night and is asleep under Grass Bridge, dreaming about Yingying. When he opens his eyes and sees her really standing there, his surprise and delight know no bounds. Having already suffered the pain of separation, the two resolve to go somewhere far, far away, where they can live happily ever after. ∎

River View Pavilion

Origin:

    Yuan Dynasty (1206-1368 AD) opera, **River View Pavilion**

Time:

    Ancient time

Place:

    Southern China

Main characters:

    Tan Ji'er (a widow, later the wife of Bai Shizhong)

    Bai Shizhong (a minor official)

    Yang Yanei (the dissolute son of a garrison commander)

Tan Ji'er is the widow of a scholar, whose husband has been dead for three years. Yang Yanei, the son of the local garrison commander, is a dissolute playboy who will stop at nothing to get what he wants. When he lays eyes on the beautiful widow Tan Ji'er, he becomes determined to have his way with her, and harasses her relentlessly. In order to escape his attentions, Tan Ji'er flees to Clear Peace Convent, and implores Sister Bai Dao to shelter her there. The kindly nun is deeply sympathetic to Tan Ji'er's plight, and protects her in every way she can.

One day, Sister Bai Dao's nephew, Bai Shizhong, arrives at Clear Peace Convent in his robes of office to visit his aunt. Sister Bai Dao knows that Bai Shizhong's wife has died, and arranges a meeting between him and Tan Ji'er. The two hit it off right away, and quickly develop strong feelings for each other. Bai Shizhong asks Tan Ji'er to marry him, and accompany him to his new post in Tanzhou. Tan Ji'er recognizes that Bai Shizhong is a good and honorable man and accepts his proposal, profoundly grateful that Heaven has seen

This clever and humorous talking clown character is a minor county official.

fit to grant her such happiness.

Yang Yanei is furious to learn that the woman he has been lusting after has unexpectedly married a lowly minor official. He goes to court and fabricates a case, claiming that Bai Shizhong has been plotting against the Emperor. Holding the Imperial sword of justice, Yang Yanei sets sail for Tanzhou to arrest Bai Shizhong. Bai Shizhong is extremely apprehensive when he learns from a friend of his imminent arrest, and has no idea what he should do. Tan Ji'er is furious to hear that Yang Yanei is plotting against her husband. She comforts Bai Shizhong, while thinking of a way to protect him. Tan Ji'er finds out that Yang Yanei will be anchoring for the night at River View Pavilion, and disguising herself as a fishing woman, sets out to intercept him.

The lecherous Yang Yanei is spending a bored and restless night alone at River View Pavilion. When a beautiful fishing woman appears and offers him some fish, he can't believe his good fortune. Slyly he importunes her to stay and drink with him. The fishing woman accepts, and introduces herself as Second Sister Zhang. She plies him with cup after cup of wine while he composes lewd verse, until finally he passes out, dead drunk. When Yang Yanei wakes up the next morning, he discovers that the Imperial sword of justice has taken flight, and is nowhere to be seen! Hastily he casts off, and soon arrives in Tanzhou. Much to his surprise, Bai Shizhong is ready and waiting for him when he docks. Brandishing the sword of justice, Bai Shizhong binds Yang Yanei and interrogates him until he confesses that he framed the case against him. As Yang Yanei is being taken away under armed guard, the beautiful fishing woman once more appears before him. Only then does he realize that "Second Sister Zhang" is none other than the woman of his lustful dreams, Tan Ji'er, the wife of lowly official Bai Shizhong.■

Spring in the Hall of Jade

Origin:

 Ming Dynasty (1368-1644 AD) novel,

 Yu Tangchun in Distress Reunited with her Lover

Time:

 Ancient time

Place:

 Shanxi Province

Main characters:

 Su San (a renowned courtesan of classical China)

 Wang Jinlong (Su San's lover)

Wang Jinlong, the son of a wealthy family, loves wine, women, and song, and spends money like water. One day in a brothel he meets renowned courtesan Su San, just Sixteen and in the first flower of her sensuality. The two fall in love at first sight, and become inextricably ensnared in passion's net. Wang Jinlong lives with Su San at the brothel for almost a year. He spends over 36,000 taels of silver to build her a house and pavilion, and showers her with clothes and jewels. And he bestows upon her a beautiful, poetic name—Yu Tangchun, which means "Spring in the Hall of Jade." When the madam of the brothel realizes that Wang Jinlong is rapidly depleting his purse, she privately warns Su San to end their relationship. But Su San is deeply in love with Wang Jinlong; how could she ever leave him? In order to force Su San to receive new clients, the madam picks a fight with Wang Jinlong, and has him evicted from the brothel.

Wang Jinlong takes shelter in an old ruined temple. Sick and destitute, he is at his last gasp when Su San discovers his whereabouts. Secretly she brings him two hundred taels of

*Su San tearfully tells Wang Jinlong of the injustice she has suffered, in **Spring in the Hall of Jade**.*

silver, and urges him to return to his home town and devote himself to his studies. Before he sets out, the two of them kneel before the altar and swear an oath—their love will last forever, and they will never abandon each other.

Su San returns to the brothel, but feigns illness every day and refuses to receive any new clients. The madam, seeing that there's no more profit to be made from her, sells her as a concubine to a rich merchant from Hongdong County named Shen Yanlin. Su San does everything she can to resist being sold, but her defiance is futile. Shen Yanlin's wife, surnamed Pi, is extremely jealous of Su San, and attempts to murder her by poisoning her food. Unexpectedly, Shen Yanlin eats the food by mistake, and dies on the spot. When Pi sees that she has killed her husband, she accuses Su San of the crime. She bribes the local officials, and Su San is sentenced to death.

As Su San is being taken to the provincial capital for the final decision on her case, one of her guards, old Chong Gongdao, sympathetically urges her to tell the judge of the injustice she has suffered. As fate would have it, this judge turns out to be none other than Wang Jinlong, who went on to pass the highest level Imperial examinations after Su San saved him. Wang Jinlong examines the original court record of the case, and realizes that it is severely flawed. Reading further, he encounters Su San's familiar name, and his heart almost stops in his chest. He looks down from the bench with bated breath, and there is Su San, pale and wasted and wearing convict's clothes. There's no mistake—the prisoner standing before him is none other than the woman who owns his heart and fills his dreams, Yu Tangchun. Wang Jinlong is speechless with shock, unable to continue his examination. Su San, in her turn, realizes that this judge to whom she is appealing for her life is none other than the lover for whom she has longed day and night, Wang Jinlong.

Judges Liu and Pan, who share the bench with Wang Jinlong, are wise in the ways of the world, and understand the relationship between Wang Jinlong and Su San from their shocked expressions. They determine that an injustice has been perpetrated, and uncover the identity of the true villain. Impartially they hand down their ruling according to the law, and Su San is freed. Having weathered disaster, Su San and Wang Jinlong are finally reunited. Filled with emotion, they recall all that they've been through, their hearts filled with deep appreciation of the truth of the saying "In life, only love is eternal."■

Liang Shanbo and Zhu Yingtai

Origin:
>   *Folk story*

Time:
>   *Ancient time*

Place:
>   *Zhejiang Province*

Main characters:
>   *Liang Shanbo (an impoverished scholar)*
>   *Zhu Yingtai (daughter of a wealthy family)*

In Shangyu County lives a beautiful and intelligent young woman named Zhu Yingtai. Zhu Yingtai loves to study, is exceedingly envious of the liberty that men have to leave their homes to study and make friends. One day she has the idea to disguise herself as a man, and go to study at a school in another county. She broaches the subject to her father, Zhu Gongyuan, but he thinks it would be very inappropriate. He's worried that his daughter would be mocked if she were to show her face in public, and thinks that even though she would be dressed as a man, the difficulties would be too great. Zhu Yingtai is very angry at her father's refusal, and mopes around the house in funk. Seeing that his daughter's heart is set on going out to study, Zhu Gongyuan finally relents and gives his consent.

Zhu Yingtai arrives at the school disguised as a man, and commences her studies. She becomes close friends with one of her classmates, a young man named Liang Shanbo. Liang Shanbo comes from a poor family. Honest and uncomplicated, he has no idea that Zhu Yingtai is really a woman, and treats her with brotherly affection. The two study together for three years, and their feelings for each other steadily deepen. One day, Zhu Yingtai receives a letter from her father, directing her to return home at the earliest opportu-

A Beijing opera ingenue, just blossoming into womanhood.

nity. Zhu Yingtai has no choice but to comply, and prepares to depart. Liang Shanbo goes to see her off, but can't bring himself to let her go down the road. Zhu Yingtai drops hint after hint about her love for him, but Liang Shanbo remains oblivious. Finally, she pretends that she has a younger sister at home, and promises her to Liang Shanbo in marriage. The two agree to meet again in the fall.

Zhu Yingtai arrives home, and discovers that her father has betrothed her to the son of local official Ma Wencai. She is unable to defy her father's orders, and plans for the marriage are finalized. Zhu Yingtai doesn't know how she's going to be able to face Liang Shanbo.

Autumn comes and Liang Shanbo is astonished and overjoyed to learn that Zhu Yingtai is really a woman. But when their hopes of marriage are burst like a fragile bubble, he falls ill with grief and dies of a broken heart.

The day comes that Zhu Yingtai is sent to the Ma family to be married. As the bridal sedan passes Liang Shanbo's grave, she insists on stopping, and gets down to make an offering. Zhu Yingtai is crying bitterly, when suddenly the earth of the grave cracks open. Without a moment's hesitation she leaps in, and is buried together with Liang Shanbo. According to the legend, the two lovers are transformed into butterflies, and fly away together wing to wing. This folk legend has been told far and wide, and is known as "China's Romeo and Juliet".∎

VII Legends about Immortals

The Goddess of Luo River

> Origin:
> *Three Kingdoms Period (220-280 AD) prose poem,*
> ***Offering to the Goddess of Luo River***
> Time:
> *Three Kingdoms Period (220-280 AD)*
> Place:
> *Northern China*
> Main characters:
> *Cao Zhi (younger brother of Emperor Cao Pi)*
> *The Goddess of Luo River*

Cao Cao's eldest son, Cao Pi, has ascended the throne and become Emperor. Cao Pi's younger brother, Cao Zhi, is exceptionally gifted and learned in many fields, and was their father's favorite. Cao Cao had attempted to have Cao Zhi designated as his heir, but was unsuccessful. As a result, Cao Pi regards Cao Zhi with suspicion and envy.

Cao Pi's wife, Empress Zhen, is graceful and elegant, with skin like snow and a face like a peach blossom. She detests her husband's cruelty and coarseness, and loves the artistic, brilliant Cao Zhi. Cao Zhi, in his turn, deeply admires Empress Zhen's intelligence and strength of character. Although it is impossible for the two to express their love, they are each aware of what is in the other's heart.

The day comes that Cao Pi, in one of his rages, has Empress Zhen put to death. When Cao Zhi learns of this, his grief is deep and bitter. He leaves the capital to return to his manor.

The Goddess of Luo River and the gifted Cao Zhi, in **The Goddess of Luo River**.

As he is passing along the banks of the Luo River, he spies a river goddess who seems to be exactly like Empress Zhen, in both appearance and spirit. He pursues her, and finally she agrees to meet him at the river the following day.

Early the next morning, Cao Zhi is waiting on the banks of the wide, misty Luo River. Suddenly, far off in the distance, he sees a heavenly cloud wafting towards him. Standing on it is a celestial figure, the Goddess of Luo River. Cao Zhi watches as she approaches like a lotus floating on the water, his eyes filled with her bright gaze and white teeth, alabaster skin and pearly lips. Reverently he bows to greet her, and asks her where she lives. She starts to speak but stops herself. Sadly she tells him that mortals and deities live in different worlds, and although fate should have brought them together, it may not be. She brings out a shining pearl, and gives it to Cao Zhi as a keepsake. Cao Zhi hastily removes the jade amulet from his belt, and offers it to the goddess with both hands. Silently, the two gaze deeply into each other's eyes, their hearts filled with inexpressible longing. The sun rises and dawn light paints the sky, and the beautiful Goddess of Luo River floats away on her cloud. ∎

Three Attacks on White Bone Demon

Origin:

*Ming Dynasty (1368-1644 AD) novel, **Journey to the West***

Time:

Tang Dynasty (618-907 AD)

Place:

Western China

Main characters:

Sun Wukong (a legendary Chinese hero)

Tang Seng (Sun Wukong's master)

White Bone Demon (a legendary Chinese demon)

Buddhist monk San Zang, known as Tang Seng, and his three acolytes—monkey spirit Sun Wukong, pig spirit Zhu Bajie, and river spirit Sha Seng—are on a pilgrimage to the Western Paradise to obtain scriptures from the Buddha. Along the way, they are faced with ten thousand trials to prove their worthiness. Fortunately, Sun Wukong has supernatural vision which allows him to recognize demons in any form, and powers that enable him to protect his master from all harm.

One day, master and acolytes are passing through the rugged peaks of high mountains. Tired and hungry, they stop to rest. Sun Wukong uses his magic golden staff to inscribe a protective circle on the ground, and tells his companions to stay inside where they will be protected from demons. He then leaps upon a magic cloud, and goes off in search of food.

Corpse spirit White Bone Demon, who has practiced her magic in these mountains for a thousand years, has been secretly following the pilgrims on their trek. She has heard that eating the flesh of Tang Seng will impart immortality, and is seeking an opportunity to get

Legendary dispeller of demons and conqueror of evil, monkey spirit Sun Wukong.

close to him. She waits until Sun Wukong is gone, and transforms herself into a young woman with a face like peach blossoms and eyebrows like willow leaves. Carrying a porcelain crock full of food, she smilingly approaches Tang Seng and his acolytes. Gluttonous and lustful Zhu Bajie heedlessly leaps out of the protective circle, and calls to his master to join him. Luckily, Sun Wukong returns from picking peaches just as the young woman is reaching for Tang Seng. Recognizing White Bone Demon through her disguise, he lets out a yell and brings his magic golden staff down upon her head. White Bone Demon is so startled that she evaporates into a wisp of smoke and flees, leaving behind a false corpse of the young woman. Not realizing the truth, Tang Seng severely rebukes Sun Wukong for killing her. Sun Wukong shows his master the porcelain crock, now filled with toads and maggots, and warns him not to let himself be tricked. Tang Seng isn't sure whether to believe him or not.

White Bone Demon flees back to her cave, gnashing her teeth, and vows that she won't give up so easily. Once more she transforms herself, this time into a wrinkled old granny, and returns to Tang Seng to demand her daughter back. The kindhearted monk, who has no idea that this is really a demon in disguise, doesn't know how to explain that the young woman is dead. But Sun Wukong is immediately aware that White Bone Demon is once more trying to trick his master, and without stopping to explain, strikes her down with his magic staff. White Bone Demon again evaporates into smoke and flees, as a second false corpse topples to the ground. Tang Seng is outraged, and furiously rebukes Sun Wukong for hurting people. He recites a special incantation, causing the golden circlet that Sun Wukong wears upon his head to constrict tighter and tighter, until he rolls on the ground in pain.

Seizing the opportunity to sow further discord between master and acolyte, White Bone Demon once more transforms herself, this time into a white haired old man. Sun Wukong sees that it is really a demon and tries to attack, but Tang Seng hastens to hold him back. Sun Wukong makes a supreme effort and breaks free, striking down the demon. White Bone Demon leaves yet another false corpse, once more tricking Tang Seng. Tang Seng can't be convinced of the truth. He refuses to forgive Sun Wukong, and sends him home to Huaguo Mountain.

Seeing that Sun Wukong is gone, White Bone Demon leads a group of demons to capture Tang Seng and the other acolytes, and holds them captive in her cave. Zhu Bajie manages to escape, and flies to Huaguo Mountain to ask Sun Wukong to return. Sun Wukong disguises himself as White Bone Demon's mother, and rescues his master and Sha Seng from the cave. In order to defeat White Bone Demon, he transforms himself into thousands of identical copies of himself, surrounding her so that she can't move. He ignites a huge conflagration, forcing White Bone Demon to revert to her true form—a pile of white bones. When Tang Seng sees this he has a great revelation, and the companions continue on their Journey to the West. ∎

The Legend of White Snake

Origin:	
	Tang Dynasty (618-907 AD) novel, **Li Huang**
Time:	
	Ancient time
Place:	
	Zhejiang Province
Main characters:	
	Bai Niangzi (a snake spirit)
	Xu Xian (a mortal man)
	Xiao Qing (a snake spirit)

On the steep and lovely slopes of E'mei Mountain live two snake spirits. One white and one grass green, they have been practicing their magic here for a thousand years. Among their many powers, they can control the rain and lightening, and transform themselves into ten thousand shapes. Curious about the richness of mortal life, they decide to transform themselves into two young women, and amuse themselves on the banks of beautiful West Lake. The white snake spirit becomes a lovely young woman, named Bai Niangzi, and the grass green snake spirit becomes her maid, Xiao Qing.

It is the time of the Festival of Clear Brightness at West Lake. A misty rain is falling, and the scenery is bewitchingly beautiful. Bai Niangzi is strolling along the lakefront when she encounters the handsome young Xu Xian. Passion floods her heart, and with Xiao Qing acting as go-between, she offers Xu Xian her eternal love. Xu Xian is overjoyed, and immediately accepts. They are married, and embark upon a life of wedded bliss.

High up in Gold Mountain Temple, head monk Fa Hai looks down and spots the telltale mist of magic rising from West Lake. Grasping his staff, he descends the mountain. He confronts Xu Xian, and tells him that his wife, Bai Niangzi, is really a snake spirit in disguise. Xu Xian is not convinced, but in order to discover the truth, he follows Fa Hai's directions and puts a special powder in Bai Niangzi's wine. Bai Niangzi is overcome by the wine and reverts to her true form, a speckled gray snake as big around as a barrel. When Xu Xian sees this, he is so horrified that he falls into a coma and cannot be roused. In order to save her husband's life, the pregnant Bai Niangzi ascends the immortal's mountain, does battle with the celestial doorkeeper, and steals the rare fungus that will revive him. Xu Xian gradually regains consciousness, but he is left with deep misgivings about his wife. Fa Hai, seizing upon Xu Xian's uncertainty, exhorts him to leave this demon spirit and take his vows in the temple.

*Snake spirits Bai Niangzi and Xiao Qing meet Xu Xian at Broken Bridge after defeating Gold Mountain Temple, in **The Legend of White Snake**.*

When three days go by and Xu Xian doesn't return home, Bai Niangzi realizes that Fa Hai has stolen away her husband. She arrives at Gold Mountain Temple with Xiao Qing and beseeches Fa Hai to release Xu Xian. But the ironhearted monk refuses, unmoved. Bai Niangzi and Xiao Qing use their magic powers to rouse the forces of the river and inundate Gold Mountain. Fa Hai responds by deploying his celestial allies, and the two forces battle to the death. Bai Niangzi is overcome with pain in her belly, and retreats to West Lake's Broken Bridge.

Xu Xian, hearing his wife's cries outside the temple, escapes from Fa Hai. He reaches Broken Bridge, and Xiao Qing rushes out with sword in hand to kill him. Xu Xian kneels before Bai Niangzi and begs

*Attractive and sophisticated Xu Xian, the young male character in **The Legend of White Snake**.*

her forgiveness, and Bai Niangzi throws herself in front of him to protect him from Xiao Qing. Forthrightly, Bai Niangzi tells Xu Xian her life story. He is deeply moved, and bitterly regrets his actions. The two reconcile, and are as happy as when they first were married.

The whole family is elated when before long, Bai Niangzi gives birth to a baby boy. But suddenly, Fa Hai appears with his immortal cohort, Jia Lan, brandishing a magic golden begging bowl. Bai Niangzi cannot evade him, and is trapped under the heavy golden bowl. Fa Hai imprisons her under the weight of Thunder Peak Pagoda in the middle of West Lake, and in the blink of an eye, husband, wife, and child are torn apart forever.

Several hundred years later, Xiao Qing returns from the mountains where she has been restoring her powers. Mustering the celestial soldiers and heavenly generals, she topples and burns Thunder Peak Pagoda, and rescues Bai Niangzi.∎

The Lotus Lantern

Origin:

    Yuan Dynasty (1206-1368 AD) opera,

    Prince Chen Xiang Cleaves Hua Mountain

Time:

    Ancient time

Place:

    Shaanxi Province

Main characters:

    Sheng Mu (Goddess of the Mountain)

    Liu Yanchang (a mountain physician)

    Chen Xiang (Sheng Mu's son)

On Hua Mountain stands an old and famous temple, where offerings are made to Sheng Mu, the Goddess of the Mountain. Every spring when the weather turns warm and the earth wakes up from its winter sleep, malarial fogs and harmful vapors fill the air, bringing great harm to plants, animals, and humans. During this season, the kind and loving Goddess of the Mountain appears carrying the magic Lotus Lantern, illuminating the entire mountain, dispelling harmful fogs and vapors, and showering blessings on the four directions.

Whenever young physician Liu Yanchang climbs the mountain to gather herbs, he always stops at the temple to silently pay homage to Sheng Mu. One day, he inscribes a poem of thanks and admiration on the scarlet fabric draped over her image. Sheng Mu is deeply moved, and steps down off the altar, as real as life. She stands before Liu Yanchang filled with tenderness, and declares her love for him.

With the help of the magical powers of the Lotus Lantern, Liu Yanchang and Sheng Mu are finally able to join together as husband and wife. When Sheng Mu's brother, the immortal Er Lang, hears that the Goddess of the Mountain has married a mortal without his permission, he is furious. Leading a force of heavenly soldiers and celestial generals, he descends and seizes Liu Yanchang. To protect her husband, Sheng Mu goes to battle with the Lotus Lantern held aloft, and defeats Er Lang.

Before long, Sheng Mu gives birth to a son, and names him Chen Xiang. Just as the family is celebrating the baby's one hundredth day, Er Lang reappears. Stealing the Lotus Lantern, he launches a new attack against Sheng Mu. Sheng Mu fights him off with her sword, while Liu Yanchang stands behind her tightly holding Chen Xiang. But without the magic lantern, Sheng Mu's strength is gradually depleted, until finally Er Lang traps her under a mountain. Er Lang tries to kill the baby, but Pili, the God of Thunder and Lightening, arrives in the nick of time and carries him away to safety.

Liu Yanchang, bereft of his loved ones, combs the peaks and valleys of Hua Mountain searching fruitlessly for his wife and child. Fifteen years go by, and Pili raises Chen Xiang up into a powerful young man, thoroughly versed in the martial arts. When Chen Xiang learns of his background, he asks Pili to release him so he may search for his father and rescue his mother. Pili grants Chen Xiang magical assistance, giving him a battle axe imbued with un- limited powers. Chen Xiang finds his father and recovers the Lotus Lantern. He defeats Er Lang, and cleaving open Hua Mountain with his magic axe, rescues his mother imprisoned within. ■

Sheng Mu, the Goddess of Hua Mountain, in **The Lotus Lantern**.

图书在版编目（CIP）数据

京剧启蒙／梁燕著. —北京：外文出版社，2003.2
ISBN 7-119-03288-7

Ⅰ．京… Ⅱ.梁… Ⅲ.京剧－剧目－简介－英文
Ⅳ.J821

中国版本图书馆 CIP 数据核字(2003)第 009401 号

外文出版社网址：http://www.flp.com.cn
外文出版社电子信箱：info@flp.com.cn
　　　　　　　　sales@flp.com.cn

总 策 划	丁　伟	Project director	Ding Wei
监　制	李　新	Supervising directors	Li Xin
	刘　燊		Liu Shen
	李沪生		Li Husheng
策　划	庄丽肖	Executive directors	Zhuang Lixiao
	刘世平		Liu Shiping
	于　苉		Yu Peng
撰　稿	梁燕	Author	Liang Yan
责任编辑	高约娜	Managing editor	Gao Yuena
装帧设计	唐少文	Graphic designer	Tang Shaowen
篆　刻	范大勇	Seal artist	Fan Dayong

出版发行：外文出版社
地　　址：中国北京百万庄大街24号
邮政编码：100037
开　　本：16开(180 × 224mm)平装
字　　数：15千字
版　　次：2003 年 4 月第 1 版第 1 次印刷
印　　数：00001－20200 册
印　　刷：鑫富华彩印
书　　号：ISBN 7-119-03288-7/G · 543（外）
定　　价：50.00 元

First edition　2003
ISBN 7-119-03228-7/G · 543
Copyright　2003
Foreign Languages Press

Published by
Foreign Languages Press
24 Baiwanzhuang Road, Beijing, China

Printed in the People's Republic of China